The Ships of
Scapa Flow

CAMPBELL McCUTCHEON

AMBERLEY

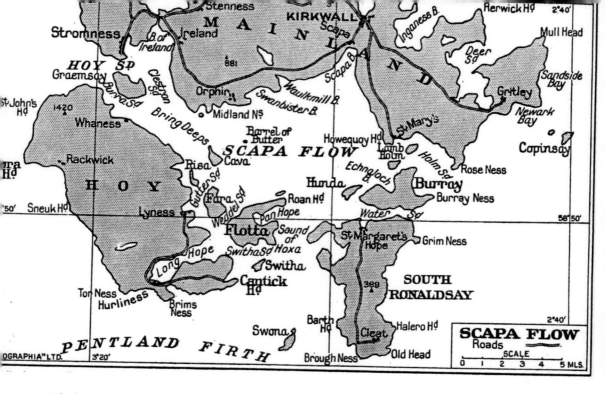

The harbour at Scapa Flow is surrounded by islands, making it a safe haven for ships.

First published 2013

Amberley Publishing
The Hill, Stroud
Gloucestershire, GL5 4EP

www.amberley-books.com

British Library Cataloguing in Publication Data.
A catalogue record for this book is available from the British Library.

ISBN 978 1 4456 3386 2
E-book ISBN 978 1 4456 3398 5

Typeset in 10pt on 12pt Sabon.
Typesetting and Origination by Amberley Publishing.
Printed in the UK.

Contents

Salvage of the German battleships and cruisers was hard work, with *Hindenburg* costing some £50,000 to raise at the time. These two views show the up-turned *Bayern* being towed up the Firth of Forth to Rosyth.

Introduction

At the start of the twentieth century, Britain and Germany began on a journey that would end with the loss of a generation on the fields of Flanders. A naval race was started that also saw one of the most prolonged periods of peacetime naval construction in history. With the development of HMS *Dreadnought*, the balance of naval power changed totally in Britain's favour and with a desire to keep Britain ahead of its neighbours, the UK began a construction programme of Dreadnoughts and cruisers to update its fleet. With the Germans and French trying to keep up, to retain its naval superiority, Britain too had to keep building new ships.

The growth of the fleet brought too a need for new naval bases that could accommodate the enlarged fleet. Both Invergordon and Rosyth were chosen and work began on facilities there for the fleet. However, by the time war started, neither was complete and Scapa, with its expanse of calm, deep water was chosen. There had been pre-war visits to Scapa by ships of the Home Fleet, but the choice of base was almost a snap decision and Scapa too was unfortified, so work began very quickly to prepare and defend the base. Minefields, shore gun emplacements and sophisticated listening stations using hydrophones, as well as concrete barriers in some of the channels, were the primary defences, although the base also developed a Royal Naval Air Station, with airships, to defend the area.

By 1916, and with the German High Seas Fleet all but blockaded in their bases of Wilhelmshaven and Kiel, the fleet moved to Rosyth, which had now been constructed. Scapa was still utilised as a base but many of the capital ships had moved to the Firth of Forth and the repair and maintenance facilities contained in the new naval dockyard. The end of the war saw Scapa become the home of the surrendered German High Seas Fleet and in 1919, it saw the biggest scuttling of a navy, and one that would not be repeated until the scuttling of the French fleet in Toulon during the Second World War.

In the Second World War, Scapa was once more used as a base. Its unique position at the approaches to the North Sea from the Atlantic gave it great strategic importance and ships based there could blockade the Germans and prevent ships from breaking out into the Atlantic. After the loss of the *Royal Oak* in 1939, more defences were created at Scapa, from concrete gun emplacements and pillboxes to the Churchill Barriers, and a comprehensive screen of anti-aircraft guns. RAF Grimsetter opened in 1940. The harbour became important as a convoy assembly point, especially for the important Arctic convoys to Russia, but also for the convoy escorts. Despite numerous air raids, Scapa was an excellent base and many thousands of sailors and merchant seamen were based there.

In 1956, with the post-war decline of the Royal Navy, Scapa was no longer needed. The threat was no longer from Germany but from Russia and the likelihood was that an invasion would take place over the German plain, rather than by sea. Scapa closed, as a result.

Nowadays, Scapa has become one of the world's premier dive sites, with its three German battleships (*Koenig, Markgraf* and *Kronprinz*), four cruisers (*Cöln, Dresden, Karlsruhe* and *Brummer*) and the destroyer V83, the focus of diving today. Scuba divers can also visit the UB-118, sunk during the First World War, and the blockships *Tabarka, Gobernador Bories* and *Doyle*. Three wrecks are war graves and cannot be dived upon. They are the *Vanguard, Royal Oak* and *Hampshire*, which between them hold the graves of some 2,200 British sailors.

Even today, despite the last ship being salvaged in 1939, parts are still removed from the German warships, due mainly to the need for high quality steel manufactured before the atom bomb era. With lower levels of radiation, this steel is important for medical purposes and is used in many MRI scanning machines.

It must not be forgotten that the salvage of the wrecks of Scapa Flow still rates as one of the most important salvage efforts of all time. Nor should it be forgotten that the naval base at Rosyth played a huge part in the recovery of those ships too. Mothballed after the First World War, Rosyth's huge dry dock was used to break up the German fleet and any salvage would have been harder without it.

This is the story of the ships of Scapa Flow, illustrated with many period photos taken by naval and private photographers, as well as postcard publishers from Orkney and further afield. Without those individuals, this book would not have been possible.

The quiet, tranquil waters of Scapa Flow hide the graves of over 1,500 British sailors, as well as the hulks of German warships scuttled at the end of the First World War.

British battleships leaving Scapa Flow for exercises in 1909 on a postcard by Thomas Kent.

Leaving the harbour at Scapa could lead to a stormy voyage, as shown on this view of the tribal-class destroyer HMS *Mohawk* on a voyage from Kirkwall to Ardrossan in 1910.

DEPARTURE OF THE GERMAN SHIPS FROM POMPEY

The period from 1897 until the start of the First World War was one of expansion for both the British and German navies. The fleets also made courtesy visits to each other's naval ports. Here, the *Scharnhorst* is leaving Portsmouth after a visit.

THE BRITISH FLEET IN KIEL HARBOUR. JUNE 1914.
ONE MONTH PRIOR TO THE WAR.   ABRAHAMS & SONS.
                                                  DEVONPORT.
"AUDACIOUS".   "AJAX".   "CENTURION".   "KING GEORGE V. (Flagship)".
"NOTTINGHAM".   "BIRMINGHAM".   "SOUTHAMPTON".

In June 1914, Britain's Dreadnought battleships, including the brand new *Audacious* which was less than ten months old, visited Kiel. A Zeppelin flies over the fleet, which in two months would be at war.

Chapter One

The World War One Wrecks:
Hampshire and *Vanguard*

Built at Elswick on the Tyne, by Armstrong Whitworth, and launched on 24 September 1903, HMS *Hampshire* was a *Devonshire*-class armoured cruiser. She spent her early career from 1905 with the Channel Fleet, before heading for the Mediterranean in 1911 and then onto the China Station. At the start of the war, she was sent back to Britain and joined the Grand Fleet at Scapa in 1915. On 31 May 1916, she took part in the Battle of Jutland and returned to Scapa afterwards. She was soon ordered to head for Archangel in Russia, with Lord Kitchener aboard. Escorted by the destroyers *Unity* and *Victor*, she set sail at 4.45 p.m. on the afternoon of 5 June 1916 into a heavy gale, which soon strengthened. Assuming no submarines would be operating, HMS *Hampshire*'s commanding officer, Captain Savill, ordered the destroyers to return to Scapa.

Riding heavy seas, *Hampshire* continued alone on her secret mission to Russia and was soon passing Marwick Head. At 7.40 p.m. an explosion caused her to heel to starboard. Within fifteen minutes, with her lifeboats on the starboard side damaged by the weather and the explosion and those on port side unable to be launched, she sank by the bow and was lost with all but twelve of her crew of over 600. It is thought that *Hampshire* had been sunk by mines laid immediately prior to Jutland by the submarine mine-layer U-75. Claims were made by a German spy that he had sabotaged the *Hampshire* and that he had escaped from the ship immediately prior to her sinking. *Hampshire* and her crew, as well as Kitchener and his staff, were lost and the wreck lies in 65 metres of water. Despite it being illegal to dive on her, a propeller and shaft were removed. They now reside at Lyness as a monument to the men who lost their lives.

HMS *Vanguard*, torn apart by an explosion while at anchor in Scapa. She had been laid down on 2 April 1908 and launched on 22 February 1909 at the Barrow-in-Furness yard of Armstrong Vickers. She had been built during the naval arms race that ultimately led to the First World War and was allocated to the First Battle Fleet at the start of the war and based at Scapa Flow. Along with twenty-three other Dreadnoughts, she saw action at Jutland but left the battle unscathed.

She would succumb not to a German shell or mine but to an internal explosion while at Scapa on 9 July 1917. Just before midnight, surrounded by other ships of the fleet, she was wrecked by a huge explosion, which tore her apart.

Commissioned on 1 March 1910, *Vanguard* was a *St Vincent*-class Dreadnought, displacing 19,560 tons and being 500 ft in length. She was powered by four Parsons turbines and was capable of 21.7 kt, with a range of 6,900 miles. She had ten twelve-inch guns in five turrets, and twelve four-inch guns, as well as three torpedo tubes.

Apart from firing at an unknown target on 1 September 1914, and from her time at the Battle of Jutland, *Vanguard* led a rather uneventful war until 9 July 1917. That day her crew had spent the afternoon practicing drill, including abandoning ship. At 6.30 p.m. *Vanguard* anchored at the northern end of Scapa Flow and her crew settled down for their evening routine. No one on *Vanguard* or the other ships of the fleet noticed anything amiss until the sky was lit by a huge explosion at 11.20 p.m. Soon chunks of *Vanguard* were raining down on other nearby vessels, with the largest section being a 5ft by 6ft piece which landed on the deck of HMS *Bellerophon*. This part had come from the central dynamo room.

A subsequent Court of Enquiry was held and called many witnesses from nearby vessels. It was concluded that a small explosion had been seen between the foremast and A turret, followed by two much larger explosions. On the balance of evidence either Magazine P or Q, or indeed both, had exploded, probably caused by the cordite overheating and spontaneously combusting. In all, 804 men died, with just two survivors. *Vanguard* lies in Scapa Flow as a memorial to one of the worst disasters in British naval history, made all the worse by probably being preventable.

The quarter deck and some of the crew of HMS *Hampshire*. Note the Marines in the foreground, behind the turret.

HMS *Hampshire*'s steam picket boat off Southsea, Hampshire.

The steam pinnace bringing some of HMS *Hampshire*'s crew ashore.

HMS *Hampshire* at Weymouth prior to the First World War. Note the pinnace at her side, and the men on painters keeping her touched up.

HMS *Oak* was built in 1912 and used almost exclusively at Scapa Flow. During the First World War, she was tender to the flagship of the Grand Fleet and shuttled backwards and forwards from the mainland to Orkney. *Oak* carried Lord Kitchener from Scrabster to Scapa before he transferred to the *Hampshire* for her ill-fated last voyage. HMS *Oak* was used during the surrender of the German fleet to transfer Admiral Meurer to HMS *Queen Elizabeth* to enact the surrender of the German fleet on 15 November 1918, and on the 20th to carry the King, Queen Mary and the Prince of Wales to see the fleet off the Firth of Forth. She was sold for scrap in May 1921.

Lord Kitchener was one of the first of the British leaders to realize the war would not be over by Christmas. He started a huge recruitment drive, which led to the pals battalions that were slaughtered at the Somme in 1916.

HMS *Vanguard* exploded at her moorings on the night of 9 July 1917. Only two of her crew survived the explosion that tore her apart. Deaths included a Japanese military attaché to Britain, Kyōsuke Eto.

Chapter Two

The Phantom Fleets

It was the sinking of the Dreadnought *Audacious* near the coast of Ireland on 26 October 1914 that tipped the balance of naval power. Britain was now numerically outnumbered by the Germans, with seventeen capital ships against nineteen, including four battlecruisers, on the German side. It was decided that a news blackout would be established and that the destruction of the *Audacious* by a mine would be covered up by, well, an audacious plan. The news was leaked that *Audacious* had been mined and taken to Harland & Wolff in Belfast to be repaired. Despite the secrecy, the passengers of the White Star liner *Olympic* had seen the stricken ship, and *Olympic* had tried and failed to tow it into shallow water. The sinking was perhaps one of the worst kept secrets of the war, but despite this, the Germans fell for the deception.

The reason for the failure of the Germans to take the reports of the sinking seriously was that *Audacious* still existed. How could this be? The answer lay with the First Sea Lord, Winston Churchill, and a crazy notion to create a fleet of naval vessels to confuse and confound the enemy.

'It is necessary to construct without delay a dummy fleet. Ten merchant vessels, either German prizes or British ships, should be selected at once. They should be distributed among various private yards not specially burdened with warship building at the present time. They are then to be mocked up to represent fast battleships of the First and Second Battle Squadrons.' So wrote Winston Churchill in a memo of 21 October 1914, barely five days before the loss of *Audacious*.

Harland & Wolff was chosen to do much of the conversion work and the requisite ships were commandeered. Five Canadian Pacific Line vessels, including the three oldest, were ordered to Belfast. They were *Mount Royal*, *Montezuma*, *Montcalm*, *Ruthenia* and *Tyrolia*. The Warren Line's *Michigan*, Ellerman's City Line's *City of Oxford*, Shire Line's *Perthshire* and RMSP's *Oruba* were all British ships, while the Hamburh Amerika Line war prize *Kronprinzessin Cecilie* was to become HMS *Ajax*. She had been captured early in the war and was not to be confused with the North German Lloyd vessel of the same name.

Mount Royal	HMS *Marlborough*
Montezuma	HMS *Iron Duke*
Montcalm	HMS *Audacious*
Ruthenia	HMS *King George V*
Tyrolia	HMS *Centurion*
Michigan	HMS *Collingwood*
City of Oxford	HMS *St Vincent*
Perthshire	HMS *Vanguard*
Oruba	HMS *Orion*
Kronprinzessin Cecilie	HMS *Ajax*
Manipur	HMS *Tiger*
Cevic	HMS *Queen Mary*

How were the ships converted? After all, the merchant ships were less than half the size of the corresponding naval vessels. It was quite simple: plans of each were ordered and the design of the naval ships was simply scaled down to fit each merchant vessel. Much of the work was done using wood and canvas. Despite the need for the ships to look like their naval counterparts from both sea and air, this was also easily achieved. With 2,000 men working on the vessels, seven were in progress by 5 November 1914. Extra funnels were added, dummy turrets made in the carpenters' shop and hoisted aboard, even new sterns created using steel plate. 34,000 tons of ballast filled the holds of the merchant ships to lower their freeboard. From a distance, they began to look just like their naval opposites, albeit a little smaller, and with no real weapons. Each was to have a crew of about forty – for they were in real danger of being sunk by the enemy. They had no bite though, only a bark.

The man who had tried to rescue HMS *Audacious* was made commodore of the phantom fleet. He was Captain Haddock, one of White Star Line's most experienced captains, and he was appointed commander of the Tenth Battle Squadron, as the phantom fleet was designated. On 4 December the first ships were ready to enter service and sailed for Scapa Flow. Four others were commandeered, including White Star's cattle carrier *Cevic*, which became HMS *Queen Mary*, and all were ready by February 1915. The name of the fleet was changed to the Special Service Squadron.

Once in service problems began to be noted – the speed of the squadron was a paltry seven–nine knots when sailing together and the issue of size was a problem, with all being to different scales. The fleet would often sail round the Orkneys as a deterrent to any U-boat commander in the vicinity. They then sailed for Loch Ewe to be worked up into a formidable 'fighting' force.

Orion (or *Oruba*) was designated as submarine bait and sent out to Rosyth. She made it safely but Admiral Jellicoe had realized the ships were effectively useless in home waters. It was decided to send some to the Dardanelles to fool the Germans. It was only a matter of time before the Germans found a dummy ship to sink and it was Brocklebank's *Manipur*, now HMS *Tiger*, which was the victim. Torpedoed by a small German submarine brought overland in pieces from Kiel and assembled at Pola on the Adriatic, she was the only war loss of the Phantom Fleet. Two firemen and two engineers were killed when the torpedo struck amidships, but the rest of the crew got off safely and were rescued close to Mudros. Two of the vessels (*Orion*, ex-*Oruba* and *Collingwood*, ex-*Michigan*) were loaded with concrete and sunk as blockships off Kephalo Bay and Mudros.

HMS *Queen Mary* was sent to the three-mile limit off America's east coast to blockade the two German commerce raiders *Kronprinz Wilhelm* and *Prinz Eitel Friedrich*. Of course, no real naval ship could be spared and it was the dummy *Cevic* that was sent to watch the two liners. On 25 April 1915, it was reported that a British battleship was off New York. There was no escape for the two German liners and they were interred for the duration. However, the usefulness of the fake battleships was becoming limited and many sailed to shipyards for conversion to oil tankers and water carriers. *Manipur* was converted into HMS *Sandhurst*, a destroyer depot ship, and survived in this role for three decades. She was the last of the dummy warships and was scrapped in 1946.

In the Second World War, there was yet again a disparity between British and German fleets, this time of age and quality. The German capital ships were all brand new, while Britain's newest ship was a decade old. Of course, this time round, a new weapon was in the navy's armoury – this was the aircraft carrier. But the Axis powers had bombers, which, as we were to find out, were more than capable of destroying a battleship. This made the North Sea unsafe.

Yet again, with not enough battleships and battle squadrons to cover its requirements, the Royal Navy looked to the ships of the Red Ensign to create a bluff. Shaw Savill & Albion were asked to provide three vessels, the *Pakeha*, *Mamari* and *Waimana* and sail them to Harland & Wolff's for conversion. *Paheka* was to become HMS *Resolution*, *Waimana* to HMS *Revenge*, while *Mamari* was to become HMS *Hermes*, a flat-top. This time, the idea was not to use the ships in active service but to create the illusion that the fleet was somewhere it wasn't. In that respect conversion was easier as the ships ideally only had to fool the pilots of the Luftwaffe. The armaments of the real battleships were painstakingly built of wood and canvas, to a scale of 5/6th, while the ships had dummy funnels and foremasts built to resemble their naval counterparts, with direction control tower and other accoutrements. As well as ballast to lower the freeboard, the holds were also filled with empty barrels to help buoyancy.

By late November 1939, the three ships, now known as Force W, were ready to sail, and off to Rosyth they went, on a four day journey from Belfast, around the top of Scotland. Steering was difficult, with the additions to the bows and sterns of each ship, but a steady course was sailed, albeit rather slowly. On 10 December, they arrived, waiting the attack by German aircraft, which would then be pounced upon by RAF Hurricanes and Spitfires. In February 1940, King George V, on his way to launch the new HMS *Duke of York* at Clydebank, inspected one of the dummy battleships. At the end of the month, the ships were moved back to Scapa, where the base endured many air raids, none of which caused damage to the three ships of Force W. In August 1940, a huge gale hit northern Britain, the worst for almost a century, and the three ships, with their heavy superstructures, bore the brunt of the winds. Dragging anchors, they were swept down the bay towards the Home Fleet, and only quick thinking saved them from running aground. The ships were then moved to Rosyth again to be laid up. By 1941, the need for merchant shipping was desperate and two ships were handed back to their owners. Both *Paheka* and *Waimana* survived the war but *Mamari*, or HMS *Hermes*, was less fortunate.

In June 1941, *Mamari* sailed in convoy for Chatham for reconversion to a merchant vessel. She was never to reach there, being wrecked off the Wold Channel after running aground on the wrecked tanker *Ahoma*, which had been sunk by mine the previous April. With two holds holed, the crew abandoned ship. Despite salvage attempts, the wreck was attacked by E-boats and torpedoed at least three times. To stop the wreck being used to hide E-boats, it was destroyed by RAF bombers. Ten direct hits saw the superstructure demolished to below the waterline. However, her mast sat proud of the water until she was cut up in 1949. The final parts were not salvaged until 1957.

Was there still a need for phantom ships? Yes! It was in the Middle East that there was a need for a new vessel. The spring and summer of 1941 were grave for the Desert Army, with defeat after defeat, and it had been suggested that HMS *Barham* be scuttled across Tripoli harbour to block the port.

In Britain, there existed HMS *Centurion*, built in 1911 and used from 1926 as a target ship. Nevertheless, she was a true battleship in looks, albeit without any weapons. Converted to oil-burning, she was capable of being operated by remote control, which was handy when you are being shot at, even if the bombs and shells are practice ones. She was laid up in Devonport. So, it was decided that she would be used to blockade Tripoli harbour, but be camouflaged to look like one of Britain's newest battleships, HMS *Anson*. She was easier to convert, of course, still looking like a battleship, and within a few weeks she was ready. Unlike Force W, she even carried real guns, even if they were just eight 40mm Oerlikon cannons and two two-pounders. Her most important weapons, though, were eight large demolition charges. Due to the chase for the *Bismarck*, instead of sailing through the Mediterranean with escorts, the ship sailed alone via South Africa for Alexandria. With the attacks on Libya and Egypt and the fall of Greece, Britain no longer controlled the Mediterranean and the idea of using *Anson* nee *Centurion* as a blockship was cancelled. However, *Centurion* was falling apart and her engines were giving problems. Hitting a storm, she lost her forward turret, and to keep up the pretence, the Navy reported she had been in action and lost a funnel.

She was sailed to Bombay for lay-up and was soon caught up in the Japanese attacks. However, the Mediterranean theatre had no capital ships and convoys needed to get to Malta and it was decided that *Centurion* would make the journey. She was laden with food, stores and ammunition and sent in convoy from Alexandria. The convoy was harried from the air on numerous occasions, with the Germans fooled into thinking *Centurion* really was a battleship. The Italians weren't fooled but someone had forgotten to mention this to the Luftwaffe.

E-boats, U-boats, aircraft and even Italian battleships tried to attack the convoy. In the midst of this action, *Centurion* sailed on, despite being hit by a bomb from a Junkers Ju 88. Severely damaged, she limped back to Port Said, where preparations were made to sink her as a blockship at the entrance to the Suez Canal. With our fortunes turned after El Alamein, she was towed into the Great Bitter Lake and laid up.

The next use she was to be put to was in the invasion of Europe, as a blockship, in a bid to create harbours. She was ordered to sail back to the UK via Alexandria, where, after running aground, she was dry-docked, patched up, had her bomb damage repaired and was stored and fueled. In May 1944, she returned to Portsmouth for the last time. She sailed for Normandy in June, her crew having a grandstand view of the D-Day landings. Explosives were set off and she settled in the water, along with a row of other vessels, creating an artificial harbour. Her hull above the water, she was turned into a casualty clearing station, her White Ensign still flying in the wind. It was the end of a great ship, sister of the *Audacious*, and the longest lasting of the phantom fleets.

Photographed from the port side of RMS *Olympic*, boats crowd round HMS *Audacious* and remove her crew as she sinks off the coast of Donegal.

HMS *Audacious* was sunk early in the war, by a mine laid by the Germans. The Canadian Pacific steamer *Montcalm* was converted into a 'dummy' of *Audacious* to fool the Germans into thinking the ship still existed. From a distance, as shown here at Scapa Flow, she was quite convincing.

Montcalm in her peacetime guise, showing just how much she had been altered.

HMS *Iron Duke* at Scapa Flow. In reality, this was the Canadian Pacific's SS *Montezuma*.

Canadian Pacific's *Tyhrenia* as HMS *Centurion*, which would in itself be turned into a dummy warship in the Second World War.

Above and below: The *Perthshire* as HMS *Vanguard*, again taken at Scapa Flow. The superstructure and turrets were all made of wood.

Above and below: At the start of the Second World War, yet again Britain resorted to the subterfuge of a dummy fleet. In the above shot not one of the three ships visible is real. Below shows HMS *Hermes*, in reality the New Zealand Shipping Co.'s *Mamari*.

The view a German reconnaissance aircraft would have had of the *Mamari*, pretending to be *Hermes*.

On the way for conversion back to a passenger ship *Mamari/Hermes* was sunk in the North Sea.

Chapter 3

The German Surrender

On 11 November 1918, an Armistice between the Allied forces and those of Germany, Austria-Hungary and their allies was agreed. One of the conditions was that the German High Seas fleet and their submarine force were to surrender. Over 200 submarines sailed for Allied ports within the following two weeks, while the surface fleet of around seventy-four vessels was to sail for Allied or neutral ports and be interned, their fates to be decided by the peace negotiations.

The ships were disarmed, emptied of ammunition and small arms and sailed for the Firth of Forth on 19 November. Rear Admiral Ludwig von Reuter commanded the fleet aboard *Friedrich der Grosse*. A massive fleet of around 250 Allied warships awaited the German ships on the 21st as they arrived in Scotland. All guns were trained fore and aft but there was no doubt the crews were ready for action. The German flags were hauled down at 3.57 p.m. and not raised again for seven months. Each ship was checked over and they sailed for Scapa Flow, the great Orkney anchorage, between 22 and 26 November. In rows, they remained at Scapa. Admiral of the Fleet Sir David Beatty took the surrender from Admiral Meurer, who had been brought to HMS *Queen Elizabeth* on the diminutive destroyer HMS *Oak*. Meurer had been captain of the SMS *Deutschland* at Jutland in 1916, and was promoted to Rear-Admiral in 1917. He commanded the German intervention in the Finnish Civil War before negotiating the terms of the surrender of the fleet.

The British, French and American fleet that awaited the Germans was prepared for action and many of the sailors wore their blast protection just in case. As it turned out, the surrender was peaceful and the subdued Germans sailed in groups from the North Sea to captivity at Scapa Flow.

The *Königsberg* arrives in British waters to negotiate the terms of the surrender of the German High Seas Fleet.

Rear-Admiral Meurer boards the *Queen Elizabeth* for the surrender negotiations. Admiral Beatty is on the far right. Beatty would take the opportunity to humiliate the Germans and referred to Meurer as a 'wretch' throughout the negotiations.

The British Grand Fleet going out to meet The Vanquished German High Seas Fleet At the Surrender November 21st 1918.

Copyright. 748.

Abrahams Devonport

Just some of the combined fleet of 250 vessels that ensured the German High Seas Fleet would surrender quietly.

Wearing both gas and flame masks, many of the British sailors mistrusted the Germans and expect them to come out fighting.

Drawn by Douglas MacPherson, on board HMS *Resolution*, the German sailors lower the Imperial battle flag on one of the battleships at sunset on 21 November 1918.

Filmed for posterity as members of the press watch, and with flags still fluttering from the aft mast, *Königsberg* at the surrender.

A line of German battleships and cruisers at the surrender.

A German cruiser passes HMS *Queen Elizabeth* on the afternoon of the surrender.

With depth charges at its stern, a British destroyer makes a sweeping turn to port with a line of five German battleships behind.

The Allied Naval Commission at Kiel ensured that the terms of the agreement of the Armistice were carried out. This included unloading all armaments and shells from the German ships before they were sent to be surrendered.

Part of the terms of surrender included the German fleet being disarmed. Taken at Wilhelmshaven, this view shows stores and ammunition being loaded during the war but the scene would not have been dissimilar as the stores were removed in November 1918.

An American War Bonds advert referring to the surrender as the greatest humiliation the world has ever known.

The German fleet surrendered and awaiting delivery to Scapa Flow.

HMS *Lion* leading a group of battle-cruisers into Scapa Flow. The German fleet was searched, and checked for contraband and any form of weapon or ammunition and then the ships were led to Scapa in groups of five or so for internment.

SMS *Moltke* newly arrived at Scapa Flow, steam still up and already being circled by one of the many steam drifters that served the ships of the Grand Fleet.

The next four images show ships newly arrived at Scapa Flow. Steam is already blowing off and the vessels are moved to their anchorages in Scapa. Many enterprising postcard publishers, from local ones such as Burrows, Thomas Kent and J. Omond and many more naval publishers, took photos of the fleet and sold them as souvenirs to the curious locals and visiting sailors. SMS *Derfflinger* as she arrived.

The cruiser *Frankfurt* passing through a line of drifters.

Another cruiser, the *Karlsruhe*, passes through the same fleet of drifters, November 1918.

Kronprinz entering Scapa Flow and making for her new home until the governments of the Allies decided what would happen to her.

Chapter Four

Scapa Flow: The Long Wait

Once the ships had all arrived at Scapa Flow many of the crews were repatriated, but those that remained kept the ships maintained, with the odd letter from home to occupy their time as they were confined to the ships.

It was a lonely life for the German sailors. Confined to their ships, with only the occasional letter for comfort, they endured an Orcadian winter and spring. As summer approached, the Peace terms were being thrashed out. What would happen to the German navy? One thing was sure: the ships were not being returned to Germany and they would be split between the Allies. Despite the possibility of gaining a sizable number of new ships, the arrangement did not suit the British. The French and Americans would acquire many new vessels and the balance of power worldwide would change. For the defeated Germans, handing over the vessels would mean they would never be able to catch up in any naval arms race again.

Von Reuter had already decided that the fleet should be scuttled and began his preparations, knowing the fleet was to be seized as soon as the Peace Treaty was signed on 23 June. In secrecy, he planned the operation with his senior officers. A secret code word was issued and the instructions were that sea cocks were to be opened, torpedo tube valves and other openings damaged in such a way that they could not be closed. On 20 June, a signal using flags was seen on *Emden*'s peak and it was answered by the other ships of the interned fleet. Next day the British First Battle Squadron exited Scapa on an exercise. Only one destroyer, a few drifters and trawlers and a solitary depot ship were left to guard the ships. Two other destroyers were being repaired also. Soon the German fleet was flying the signal again, which translated as 'Paragraph 11, Confirm', the code for 'sink all ships immediately'. It would be the beginning of the end of the naval arms race that had led to war. For the Germans it would be a blessing as they would finally escape the damp, cold Orkneys and be repatriated back to Germany.

In neat lines, the German ships remained at anchor for months.

The battle cruisers, December 1918.

GERMAN WARSHIPS INTERNED IN SCAPA FLOW   J. OMOND

An airship station was located at Scapa Flow and it ensured that images could be taken from altitude of the rows of German ships. These two views by Kirkwall publisher J. Omond are taken over the airship base looking towards the German ships.

GERMAN WARSHIPS INTERNED IN SCAPA FLOW J. OMOND. C.

The ships at Scapa were for the most part sorted and the destroyers were mainly located together. These views give an idea of the sheer number of ships the Germans had surrendered.

Another view of the serried ranks of German battleships.

The battleship *Baden* was 623.5 ft in length and was virtually brand new when she was surrendered, having entered service in 1917. After scuttling, she was raised in 1921 and used as a target and sunk that same year.

The light cruiser *Bremse* was designed with a mainmast that could be lowered so that she could be disguised as an *Arethusa*-class cruiser of the Royal Navy. She was built in 1916 as a minelayer cruiser. Her sister ship *Brummer* was also scuttled at Scapa Flow.

A replacement for the *Nürnburg* sunk at the Battle of the Falklands, this *Nürnburg* was completed in 1916 and was 496 ft in length, and had a crew of 500.

One of the *Kaiser*-class of battleships, the *Prinz Regent Luitpold* was one of a class of five, all of which were scuttled at Scapa Flow.

SMS *Derfflinger* took part in the Battle of Dogger Bank and Jutland. With a crew of 1,214, she was 689 ft in length and had eight 12 in guns.

The light cruiser *Cöln* was built in 1918 at Blohm und Voss. Of a class of ten cruisers, seven were launched but only *Dresden* and *Cöln* were completed. Seven hulls were scrapped and the three on the stocks cut up where they lay.

Baden was one of the most powerful of the German battleships, fitted with eight 15 in guns. Her sister was the *Bayern*, which was raised and scrapped between 1934 and 1935.

Markgraf was one of four sister ships of the *Koenig* class of dreadnoughts. The other vessels, all 580ft in length and with ten 12 in guns, were *Koenig, Grosser Kurfürst* and *Kronprinz Wilhelm*.

Chapter 5

That Sinking Feeling

With the results of the Peace terms almost announced, the German commanders decided their ships would not be used as pawns in the international negotiations. It suited Britain that the ships would not head off elsewhere to change yet again the balance of naval power. The day chosen by the Germans for the sinking of their fleet was also the day the British navy sailed from Scapa on an exercise. Whether this was deliberate or a happy coincidence, it left the German sailors to their own devices and with the ability to ensure the ships would be gone by the time the British fleet returned.

The first signs of action began at about 11.45 a.m. as sailors from the *Friedrich der Grosse* began to throw their belongings into rowing boats. *Frankfurt*'s sailors were doing the same. It was obvious the ships were beginning to sink and a message was sent to the Battle Fleet to return to Scapa, as the trawler *Sochosin* went to the *Frankfurt* to find out what was happening. Soon, many of the fleet were slipping under the waters of Scapa. However, the depot ship *Sandhurst* and numerous trawlers and drifters managed to beach eleven destroyers, while the battleship *Baden* and two cruisers lay in shallow water in Swinbister Bay, with another light cruiser off Cava. A group of Orcadian schoolchildren, aboard the *Flying Kestrel*, were on a trip round the fleet and were caught in the action as the ships went down around them.

Men from the *Westcott* managed to board the *Hindenburg* but water was sloshing around inside and it was soon obvious it was getting deeper and deeper. Explosives were used to break her anchor chain and she started to drift to shore. She was soon under tow but once in shallow water she beached and turned turtle. From the *Hindenburg*, *Westcott* went to the *Nürnberg* to try to save her, slipped her anchor and watched her drift ashore.

By 2.30 p.m., the first destroyers had returned to find only two battleships, one battle cruiser and four light cruisers still afloat, with the once neat lines of warships nowhere to be seen, with some beached or upside down in the shallow water. While the few ships were still afloat, they were sinking too. The day after only *Baden*, three cruisers and eighteen destroyers were above the waters of Scapa. The rest of the fleet would no longer pose a menace to Allied shipping, nor would it be of use to the Allies and Britain remained the supreme naval power in the Atlantic.

The Admiralty decided that the ships could not be salvaged and that, as most posed no threat to navigation, they would remain in Scapa Flow. By the mid-1920s, it was obvious the ships were a danger to shipping, both naval and the many trawlers in the vicinity. The glut of wartime scrap had already been used up too and there was a demand for quality steel scrap for the steel furnaces of the world. Some enterprising Orcadian farmers and fishermen had already relieved the more accessible vessels of any easily recovered non-ferrous scrap but there still remained hundreds of thousands of tons of high quality metal in Scapa.

On the morning of 21 June 1919, a group of Orcadian schoolchildren were given a grandstand view of the fleet sinking. They were on a Sunday School trip around the fleet on the tug tender *Flying Kestrel*. Unwittingly, they were caught up in one of the most spectacular events ever to occur in the Orkneys. This extremely rare postcard shows the battleship grey *Flying Kestrel* returning to Kirkwall with the schoolchildren crowding her deck after the scuttling. The *Flying Kestrel* herself was also one of the tugs which attended the RMS *Queen Mary* when she was launched in 1934.

Bayern sinking.

Seydlitz, as she had appeared in the morning of 21 June 1919.

Seydlitz on her side, with two sailors on her port side.

Another view of *Seydlitz*, showing her upper decks. She was the flagship of the High Seas Scouting Force and took part in the Battles of Dogger Bank and Jutland. She had ten 11 in guns and was some 656 ft in length.

3.45 p.m. and with *Baden* still afloat, next to her cruisers are still sinking, while two have turned turtle.

German sailors from scuttled ships aboard a British destroyer. Nine germans would die in the scuttling, all from British gunfire, and would become the last casualties of the First World War.

Boatloads of German sailors approach HMS *Ramilles*. Their belongings were thrown into the small boats as their ships sank underneath them.

German officers aboard HMS *Ramilles*.

Above and below: Some of the ships were run aground, while others were sunk in shallow water. These images show SMS *Hindenburg* with her funnels and superstructure above water. Completed in May 1917, she was raised between 1930-32 and scrapped at Rosyth.

Chapter 6

Salvage

The first ship, a destroyer, was recovered in 1922 by the Stromness Salvage Syndicate and cut up in Stromness. Novel uses were found for the boiler tubes, which when polished up became curtain rods. In June 1923 a new syndicate bought some of the vessels and began work to recover them using concrete barges. The barges were connected with girders and chains placed around the destroyers. Slowly, they would be lifted clear of the bottom. Another man intent on salvage was Ernest Frank Guelph Cox. He visited the area and looked at the vessels, announcing he had bought over twenty vessels, including *Hindenburg* and *Seydlitz*. Salvage operations would begin on these vessels quite quickly and Cox used the naval base at Lyness, from where operations could be controlled. Cox, from Dudley, had made his money during the war, when his factory made shell cases. He had started shipbreaking in 1921 with the purchase of HMS *Orion* and *Erin*, which he broke up in Queensborough. In the yard was a German floating dock, with a pressure-testing cylinder for submarines, and with a lift of 3,000 tons. The tube was sold and the dock transported to Lyness. Two tugs, the *Ferrodanks* and *Sidonian*, were also bought off the Admiralty. When it arrived at Lyness, one side of the dock was cut away so that it created a floating platform that could be used to salvage the ships.

The small destroyers were the first ships to be recovered. Most were in shallower water and they could be salvaged with ease. The first, *V70*, was of 924 tons and lay in less than 50ft of water a mere ½ mile from Lyness. The dry dock was berthed beside the *V70* and lifting began. The principle would be that *V70* would be lifted on each tide about ten feet and transported to shallower water until she was ashore. Unfortunately, there was an issue with the chains used to lift her and she had to be placed back into the water again and new 9 in-thick hawsers replaced the 3 in chains. On 31 July 1924 another attempt was made to lift *V70*. This one was successful and after four lifts she was ashore. The price of scrap had fallen so *V70* was made watertight and renamed *Salvage Unit No.3*.

With two salvage teams working in Scapa Flow, competition between them was fierce. However, Cox & Danks were more successful, raising their third destroyer on 29 August 1924, the same day as Robertson's syndicate raised its first. By 13 November, Robertson had raised three destroyers and Cox a few more. During the winter of 1924/25, Robertson suffered damage to his concrete barges and after a fourth ship had been raised he gave up on salvage. Within twenty months, twenty-four ships had been raised, with one, *S65*, being lifted in four days. The Germans had done their work correctly when the ships were scuttled, with major damage to sea cocks, all watertight doors opened, portholes left open, all valves open or damaged and even the toilet plumbing damaged. Some of the vessels salvaged were transported to Rosyth for breaking while others were cut up on site.

As work slowed on the destroyers, the locations of the capital ships were marked and preparations began for their salvage too. *Hindenburg* was upright in 70 ft of water. She had been built between 1913 and 1917 and had not seen action at Jutland. The salvage effort on the battleships and cruisers was more tricky and each would be raised by sending divers in to the wrecks to close and seal any openings, then compressed air would be pumped in to give the ships buoyancy, from which they should rise out of the water and be towed away for scrapping. As she was being salvaged during an Orcadian gale, destroyer *G38* was blown against the floating dock, which was damaged, causing *Hindenburg* to be completely flooded once more. Partially raised by late August, she was free of the bottom in September but another gale saw the pumps damaged and *Hindenburg* back underwater, after £30,000 had been spent raising her so far. Next to be salvaged was *Moltke*, actually upside down but above water most of the time. Holes were sealed and compressed air pumped into the hull. Using huge air locks, the men could enter a ship even when sunken and this process became the way of salvaging the big capital ships. Inside the ships, even underwater, the men could work in an environment of compressed air, patching holes, closing valves, hatches and portholes. By June 1927, *Moltke* was afloat and was towed to Lyness, before being readied for the tow to Rosyth, where she would be cut up. In May 1928, the weather was deemed good enough to risk the tow. *Motlke* reached Rosyth despite a perilous journey and was scrapped in the dry dock there.

Between 1930 and 1939, as large number of vessels were lifted and broken for scrap, the last being *Derfflinger*, which was raised in July 1939 and generated 20,000 tons of scrap. *Prinz Regent Luitpold* was the last ship raised by Cox, the salvage work being taken over in 1933 by Metal Industries Ltd. They had soon purchased *Baden* and *Bayern* from the Admiralty, with *Grosser Kurfürst* costing them £2,000 to buy. *Friedrich der Grosse* grossed £134,886 in scrap so the purchase expense was minimal in terms of the real cost of raising one of the vessels. It was not only the war which saw operations cease but that most of the easily accessible ships had been raised. The feat of raising the others was too great and the depths too deep to justify the expense and danger of salvage. Remaining in Scapa are the *Dresden, Kronprinz Wilhelm, Markgraf, Koenig,* Cöln*, Karlsruhe and Brummer* as well as the destroyer *V83*, which was raised, then used during the salvage work and subsequently abandoned.

As well as the scuttled German ships, Scapa is also home to the *Royal Oak*, sunk in 1939 by a daring U-boat captain called Gunter Prien. She is now a registered war grave and dives are not allowed on her. The First World War HMS *Vanguard*, blown up at anchor, remains too as a war grave. However, a large tourist industry has grown up around the German fleet and the blockships placed in Scapa to prevent another U-boat attack. Occasionally, some metal is still salvaged from the German vessels due to the non-radioactive metal found aboard them. Post-1945, the world had changed and all metals produced subsequently have had a slight radioactive trace, and the metals from the sunken navy have proved invaluable in sensitive measuring equipment. Today, the raising of the ships at Scapa has proved to be one of the most interesting salvage attempts of all time, with over sixty vessels beached or salvaged in the twenty years from the sinking until the start of the Second World War. Eight still remain, mainly capital ships, forming the sunken navy of Scapa Flow.

An early method of salvage was to attach canvas air bags or 'camels' either side of a destroyer and use these to refloat it.

The *Nürnberg* after raising. She was one of the first of the larger ships to be raised from the waters of Scapa Flow and is shown here at 2 p.m. on 3 July 1919, barely two weeks after she had been scuttled. The shallow waters of the harbour left a reasonable number of ships either just below the surface or resting on the bottom with upper works still accessible, even at high tide.

A W. Hourston postcard of a destroyer being salvaged.

Much work on rescue and salvage was undertaken on the days of the scuttling and immediately afterwards. The crew of HMS *Violent* rescued this TBD from scuttling.

The firm of Cox & Danks salvaged most of the vessels reclaimed from the water of Scapa Flow. This view shows the first destroyer the company lifted from the water. This one took six weeks to lift as the company experimented with ways of lifting the vessel.

By the time *S55* was raised, the company was bringing destroyers up every four or five days. Despite being in 40 feet of water, *S55*'s torpedo tubes, valuable non-ferrous metal, had mysteriously disappeared despite five years in the water.

The larger ships, the cruisers and battleships, required different methods of being raised. Divers would seal any holes in the ship and then compressed air would be pumped in to make the inside fit for men to work in. This required huge airlocks, which would be attached to the upturned hull and would be used to pump compressed air into the inside of each vessel. This is the first airlock to be used on one of the German ships, which would be transported from Lyness by the tug *Sidonian* to the wreck.

Salvage was dramatic and when a ship was ready to be raised, it would break the surface in a rush of water. *Seydlitz*, shown here, was in 50 feet of water and was fitted with 60ft airlocks. Once a large ship was salvaged, the airlocks would be removed, leaving a small cap where they had once been; a hut was erected on top of the vessel and it would be towed to Rosyth for breaking up.

Seydlitz safely afloat, with the tugs *Ferrodanks*, *Sidonian* and *Bertha* to her right.

Salvage work being undertaken on SMS *Baden*. A funnel of the *Hindenburg* is to the immediate right of the salvage tug.

After a decade underwater, the *Kaiser* was raised in 1929.

With the salvage tug *Ferrodanks* to her right and one half of an ex-German floating dry dock at her left, *Bremse* is being salvaged. Note the three airlocks, all numbered, and the huge crane on the dry dock. The pulleys along the side of the dry dock were used for the cables that would raise the destroyers that Cox & Danks salvaged.

Another view of the salvage showing airlocks being fitted to one of the German ships, possibly *Hindenburg*. The pontoon crane holds the airlock as it is attached to the ship. On the extreme right airlock a diver is ready to go inside the ship.

Prinz Regent Luitpold surfaces from the deep. Fitted with both 40 ft and 60 ft airlocks, she was soon dispatched to Rosyth for final demolition.

Once raised, each ship was taken into shallower water and the tricky job of cutting away the superstructure took place. This was because the cill of the dry dock in Rosyth was not deep enough to accommodate the superstructure and because the upturned ships needed to be placed on blocks once in the dry dock. This is *Prinz Regent Luitpold* on 9 July 1931.

This would be a typical scene at Rosyth after a ship had been dry docked and immediately before final cutting up would take place.

Above and below: Prinz Regent Luitpold being towed under the Forth Bridge on her final journey.

Tugs of the Dutch company Christian Smit were used for the long tow from Orkney down the North Sea to Rosyth and many hundreds of people came out to watch each ship as it arrived for breaking.

The SMS *Motlke* is partially raised and work has already begun on the cruiser on its side astern of her. Note the years of growth of seaweed on the hull and that the offside port propeller has already been salvaged.

A lot of the seaweed was cleared so men could walk up and down the deck easily. In this view of *Moltke*, taken a short while afterwards, both her port propellers have been removed. These would have been of phosphor bronze or similar alloy and were worth their weight in gold.

As tugs crowd round her, men swarm the deck of *Moltke*, which has now been totally cleared of seaweed and had the huts built for the deck crew for the tow to Rosyth.

An unknown battleship at Rosyth.

Above and below: Bayern photographed from the Forth Bridge as she passes underneath, with the tugs *Zwarte See, Witte Zee* and *Ganges*.

Zwarte Zee towing *Bayern* into Rosyth on 30 April 1935.

By 1935 Metal Industries had taken over from Cox & Danks. Their name is emblazoned on the hut atop the upturned hull of *Bayern*.

With the hammerhead cranes of Rosyth dockyard in the background, *Bayern* is towed over the dock entrance.

Photographed from one of the tugs, *Bayern* is seen at the dock entrance. There was only some 40 ft of freeway at high tide so all obstructions had to be removed. Sometimes a diver was required at Rosyth to remove any obstructions as the ship was entering dock.

A Navy officer watches as *Bayern* comes into the dockyard at Rosyth.

Schoolchildren watch as the *Bayern* arrives. Note the difference between the ocean-going Dutch salvage tugs and the smaller one at *Bayern*'s bow.

Bayern in dry dock. Here, it is possible to see just how much of the superstructure and turrets have been removed. This is immediately after the dry dock has been emptied and water still pours from the stern of *Bayern* as she empties of water for the first time in over a decade. This view is taken from half way down the dry dock.

Photographed from the top of the dry dock, *Bayern* is ready to be cut up. Note the props to stop *Bayern* tipping over in dock.

Towing *Von Der Tann* to Rosyth.

König Albert in the process of being cut up. At the same time as she was being dismantled in Rosyth, Britain was sending wartime destroyers to Germany for scrapping.

A superb view of the SMS *Hindenburg* from above.

A stern view of *Hindenburg* in the Forth. Note just how low she is in the water.

Above and below: Two views of *Hindenburg* as she makes her final approaches to Rosyth. Once past the Forth Bridge, a sharp turn was required to enter the dockyard.

Hindenburg being towed by the tug *Seefalke*.

With the tug *Simson* at her side, *Hindenburg* passes under the Forth Bridge.

A superb view of *Hindenburg* with the Hamburg-based salvage tug *Pontos*.

Crowds have gathered to witness the *Hindenburg* entering Rosyth dockyard.

Above and below: Before the road bridge was built, it was only possible to cross the Firth of Forth by rail or by ferry. Here, the Dumbarton-built ferry *Queen Margaret* passes the *Grosser Kurfürst* and the salvage tug *Zwarte Zee* as they head for Rosyth on 29 April 1938. Note just how many vehicles crowd the deck of the ferry.

Above and below: With Dutch salvage tugs on either side, *Grosser Kurfürst* is photographed from the Forth Bridge.

Above and below: With both bow and stern shots, it is possible to see just how much clutter there is on the decks of the *Grosser Kurfürst*. The experience of sailing down the North Sea aboard could not have been a pleasant one.

Grosser Kurfürst was one of the last of the German ships to be salvaged before the war. It had been an epic salvage effort and one of the biggest in maritime history.

After twenty years of salvage, the last of the ships to be recovered was *Derfflinger*. She was raised in July 1939 and, because of the war, was not broken up until 1946. Unlike most of the other battleships and cruisers, she went from Rosyth to Faslane on the Clyde to be dismantled.

Chapter seven

The Mighty Oak

Launched in 1914 as a replacement for the 1892 *Royal Sovereign*-class ship of the same name, the *Royal Oak* was a *Revenge*-class battleship. Not completed until 1916, she was finished in time for the Battle of Jutland and made her fighting debut there, hitting the *Derfflinger* three times, putting a turret out of action. *Royal Oak* also damaged the cruiser SMS *Wiesbaden* and was straddled by at least one salvo during the battle. On 5 November 1918, while anchored in the Firth of Forth off Burntisland, a sudden storm blew the ex-Cunard ship and converted aircraft carrier HMS *Campania* into *Royal Oak* and then HMS *Glorious*. *Campania*, holed by *Royal Oak* and sinking, would slip under the waves without loss of life five hours after the initial collision. After the German surrender, *Royal Oak* escorted some of the enemy battleships to Scapa and was present as many more arrived.

Designed to be coal-fired, the *Royal Oak* was laid down at Devonport on 15 January 1914 and the shipyard was ordered to change her engines from coal- to oil-fired boilers. Equipped with eighteen Yarrow boilers, she was equipped with four turbines, powering her four propellers. Launched on 17 November 1914, she was ready for service on 1 May 1916 and had cost some £2.5 million to build.

Between the wars, *Royal Oak* was assigned to the Atlantic, Home and Mediterranean fleets. Refitted in 1926, she was sent to Malta, and in 1928, a dispute between her captain, Kenneth Dewar, and Rear-Admiral Bernard Collard saw relations between the two men collapse. Eventually, the pair, and *Royal Oak*'s second in command, Commander Henry Daniel, were returned to England, with a major naval exercise being postponed as a result. Dewar and Daniel were court-martialed for writing subversive documents, while Collard was forcibly retired from the service. The ship was refitted in 1922–24 and again in 1927, with the addition of extra anti-aircraft guns and the removal of 6-in guns from her shelter deck. Her final refit would take place between 1934 and 1936, when her deck armour was increased and a catapult for a float plane added.

During the Spanish Civil War, *Royal Oak* was in the Mediterranean and spent much time on non-intervention patrols around the Spanish Coast. On 2 February 1937, while 30 miles east of Gibraltar, she was attacked by three aircraft of the Republican forces. Three bombs landed close but caused no damage. A complaint was then made to the Spanish. While off Valencia on the 23rd of the same month, she was struck by an anti-aircraft shell, with five men being injured, including Captain Drew. In May 1937, she escorted the SS *Habana*, which was full of refugees, to Britain.

By 1938, *Royal Oak* had returned to the Home Fleet and was based in Portsmouth. The following year, it was planned for her to have a thirty-month tour of the Mediterranean but the start of war in September saw her in Scapa Flow instead. As war was declared, she was at anchor in the Orkneys. In October, she took part in the search for the *Gneisenau*, which had broken out of Germany and was heading up the North Sea. *Royal Oak*, with a top speed of 20 kt, was soon left behind by the rest of the fleet. On 12 October, she returned to Scapa, suffering damage from the search in gale-force storms. Scapa itself had been abandoned by the Navy after an overflight of a German reconnaissance aircraft, with the ships heading for other bases. The assumption was that the base would soon be attacked. *Royal Oak*'s anti-aircraft guns were thought to be a boost to the base's rather poor defenses.

Blockships had been placed at strategic points on the entrances into Scapa during and after the First World War and at least two submarines, the U-18 and UB-116, had attempted to enter the harbour during the war. U-18 was rammed twice on 23 November 1914, and her crew captured, while on 28 October 1918, UB-116 was sunk with all hands after being detected by hydrophone. Soon after the Second World War started, Scapa again saw block ships being sunk to prevent enemy submarines entering the harbour.

An attack on Scapa, however, would displace the British Home Fleet, and would make it easier for German ships to escape the North Sea and enter the Atlantic. Scapa had also been where the German fleet had been scuttled and the success of an attack there would in some way help the Germans avenge this part of their naval history. Commander of Submarines Karl Dönitz planned an attack on Scapa and hand-picked one of his best young submarine captains, Gunther Prien, with the U-47 to make a daring and possibly suicidal mission to cause havoc in the harbour at Scapa.

The reconnaissance flight, by Siegfried Kneyemer, revealed the lack of defenses, as well as a lack of viable targets in Scapa but that it was possible to enter Scapa and hopefully get round the defenses, such as they were. Prien was directed to enter the harbour via Kirk Sound, passing to the north of Lamb Holm on the attack, scheduled for high tide on the moonless night of 13–14 October 1939. Prien undertook the attack, initially mistaking Skerry Sound for his intended route and had to quickly about turn before running ashore or worse, colliding with a blockship. That night, moonless as it was, did have a spectacular show of the Aurora Borealis, visible to Prien and his deck crew as the submarine threaded its way past the blockships *Seriano* and *Numidian*, briefly being trapped in a cable strung from the *Seriano*. A moment of panic ensued as the sub was caught on the surface by the lights of a taxi ashore but either the taxi driver did not notice or he thought it was a British submarine, as no alarm was raised. It was 00.27 on the morning of the 14th as Prien's submarine finally escaped the treacherous narrows and entered the harbour proper, he entered the statement '*Wir sind in Scapa*

Flow' in the ship's log and set off into the harbour. After a couple of miles, he turned back to survey the natural harbour to discover that it was nearly empty. The ships he had been told to sink were nowhere to be seen, scared by the reconnaissance flight of a few days previous.

On the reverse course, a crewmember spotted a ship of the *Revenge*-class, with another vessel behind, which was incorrectly identified as a battleship of the *Renown*-class. The *Revenge*-class ship was obviously *Royal Oak* but the vessel behind was the *Pegasus*, built as HMS *Ark Royal*, the world's first aircaft carrier, which had seen action in both the Mediterranean and in Murmansk, Russia, during the First World War. She was renamed in 1934 as HMS *Pegasus* and was eventually scrapped in 1950. First spotted some 4,400 yards away, three torpedoes were fired at the *Revenge*-class ship at 00.58. The Germans were going through a bad patch with their torpedoes and only one exploded, at 01.04, striking the bow of the *Royal Oak* and startling her crew into action. The starboard anchor was lost and checking of the temperature of the magazines was ordered but many sailors simply went back to sleep.

Using her stern tube, U-47 let go a torpedo but this too failed to go off and soon the submarine had turned round and, with her forward tubes reloaded, fired another salvo. One tube had been blocked by a torpedo which had lodged there, so three tin fish were fired. At 01.16, all three hit, one after another, causing the armoured deck to be pierced, destroying the messes and setting alight cordite in one of the magazines. This caused a huge fireball inside the ship, killing many. At 01.29, *Royal Oak* slipped beneath the waves, having capsized on her starboard side with the loss of 833 men and boys. Over 100 of the victims were boy seamen, not yet eighteen.

Rear-Admiral Henry Blagrove, commander of the Second Battle Sqaudron was lost too and his gig, moored next to the *Oak* was also lost. Alongside the *Royal Oak*'s port side was the tender *Daisy 2*, which was quickly cut free as the ship began to capsize. *Daisy 2*'s crew managed to rescue some 386 men from the freezing waters of Scapa Flow. The thick fuel oil covering the surface caused many men to choke and die, and preventing them from swimming to shore, half a mile away. Rescue efforts continued until about 4 a.m., by which time the *Daisy 2* had collected most of the survivors and delivered them to HMS *Pegasus*. The commander of *Daisy 2*, John Gatt RNR, received a Distinguished Service Cross for his part in the rescue, the only British award made in connection with the sinking.

At first, it was thought that the *Royal Oak* had suffered an explosion in her magazines or perhaps an attack by enemy aircraft but it was soon realised the cause must have been a submarine and steps were made to prevent its escape from the anchorage. It was far too late and Gunther Prien had already successfully navigated the U-47 out of Scapa. Navy divers were soon on the scene and recovered the remains of a German torpedo and on 17 October it was announced by Winston Churchill, then First Lord of the Admiralty, that a stunning German attack had been the cause of the sinking. He stated it had been 'a remarkable exploit of professional skill and daring' but that the disaster to such an old ship would not affect the balance of sea power. It was the end, however, of the use of boy sailors on capital ships.

Quick to make propaganda of the raid, the Germans were soon crowing about their success and upon arrival of the U-47 back in Wilhelmshaven on 17 October, Prien was awarded the Iron Cross First Class and the rest of his crew an Iron Cross Second Class. The planner of the raid, Dönitz, was promoted to Rear-Admiral and made Flag Officer of U-boats.

The effects of the sinking have had a profound effect on Orkney itself. Churchill ordered the eastern defences of Scapa to be blocked. What were to become the Churchill Barriers were built. These causeways were mainly constructed by Italian prisoners and effectively blocked Prien's route as well as the gaps between Lamb Holm, Glimps Holm, Burray and South Ronaldsay. A road was built atop the barriers and it now forms the route of the A961.

Prien went on to become one of the most decorated of all the German U-boat captains but was probably lost on 7 March 1941 when HMS *Wolverine* and HMS *Verity* attacked a submarine, which exploded off the west of Ireland. Continual taunting by the British eventually forced the Germans to admit over two months later that Prien and his crew were lost.

The *Royal Oak* herself is now a designated war grave, the task of removing many of her crew being impossible under wartime conditions. She lies within 5 metres of the surface at points and her brass name letters, removed in the 1970s before she was protected as a war grave, now grace the walls of the Scapa Flow Visitor Centre at Lyness. Each year, naval divers leave a White Ensign at her stern. The ship's bell resides at the memorial to those lost in Kirkwall cathedral and some bodies which were recovered from the oily waters of Scapa Flow are buried at Lyness.

One lasting legacy of the sinking has been the almost constant seeping of oil from the wreck into the pristine waters of Scapa Flow. In 2010, after many surveys and some four years of work, Briggs Marine recovered 1,600 tons of fuel oil from the *Royal Oak*.

The sinking of the *Royal Oak* changed the very geography of Scapa Flow. Without her loss, the barriers that now connect many of the islands to the mainland of Orkney would probably not have been built. Scapa Flow has benefitted greatly from the sinking of various ships there. With both HMS *Vanguard* and *Royal Oak* being designated war graves, they cannot be dived on, but the remaining German ships from the First World War attract divers from all over the world, and Scapa Flow provides high quality diving for beginners and expert alike.

HMS Royal Oak as built in 1916, just in time for the Battle of Jutland, where she damaged SMS *Derfflinger*.

Nick-named the *Mighty Oak*, the ship saw action at Jutland and in the Middle East in 1920.

Above: At the end of the First World War, *Royal Oak* was rammed by the seaplane carrier *Campania*. Within five hours *Campania* was gone.

Opposite: Royal Oak in a heavy sea.

Royal Oak in the Mersey, on a rare visit to Liverpool. Note the crew on deck.

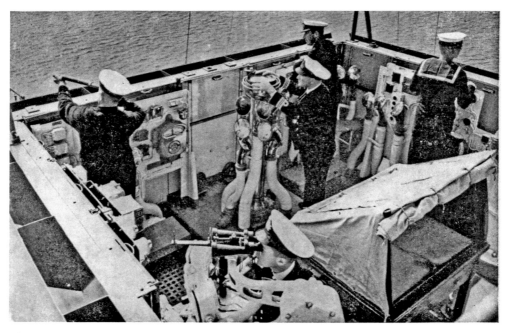

The navigation bridge of *Royal Oak*. One of the officers is taking a sight from the box compass.

Off Weymouth when at Portland. On the port view, *Royal Oak* is being painted.

A rather poor image showing *Royal Oak* in dry dock, probably at Scapa Flow.

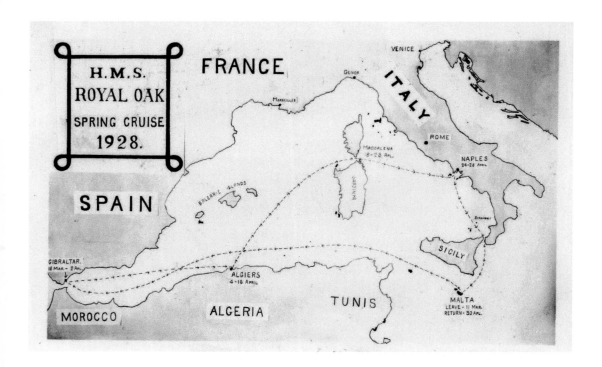

ITALY

GREECE

SICILY

MUDROS
24 JLY – 1 AUG

SKIATHOS
11 – 23 JULY

ARGOSTOLI
11 – 22 AUG.

NAVARIN
29 JUN – 10 JUL.

MILO
2 – 10 AUG

MALTA
LEAVE – 27 JUNE
RETURN – 24 AUG.

H.M.S. ROYAL OAK
FIRST PART SUMMER CRUISE 1928

Above and opposite, below: In 1928, when in the Mediterranean, *Royal Oak*'s captain and first officer fell out with the officer commanding the squadron. This led to all three being removed from their posts and the Rear-Admiral being forcibly retired.

Four German U-boats; among them is U-47, the submarine of Gunther Prien, Germany's most successful U-boat captain.

Behind *Royal Oak* was HMS *Pegasus*, which had been the *Ark Royal*, built as a seaplane carrier during the First World War. The survivors were taken aboard *Pegasus* after *Royal Oak* sank.

After the daring raid, more blockships were sunk in Scapa Flow, including the SS *Ilsenstein*, shown here being sunk in 1939.

Using mainly Italian prisoners of war, the Churchill Barriers were built to block many of the entrances to Scapa Flow. A road now runs over the barriers, connecting the islands to the mainland of Orkney. They are a lasting legacy of the tragedy of HMS *Royal Oak*.

Lest we forget 1! The planner of the raid on the *Royal Oak* was Karl Dönitz, shown here at the left end of the second row at the Nuremburg War Trials. Hermann Goering is directly in front of him.

Lest we forget 2! Two crew members of HMS *Royal Oak*.